JUMP START YOUR ROAD TO RICHES
MAXIMIZE YOUR PROFITS WITH PENNY STOCK TRADING

BY: KEN ROBBINS

© Copyright 2016 - All rights reserved.

In no way is it legal to reproduce, duplicate, or transmit any part of this document in either electronic means or in printed format. Recording of this publication is strictly prohibited and any storage of this document is not allowed unless with written permission from the publisher. All rights reserved.

The information provided herein is stated to be truthful and consistent, in that any liability, in terms of inattention or otherwise, by any usage or abuse of any policies, processes, or directions contained within is the solitary and utter responsibility of the recipient reader. Under no circumstances will any legal responsibility or blame be held against the publisher for any reparation, damages, or monetary loss due to the information herein, either directly or indirectly.

Respective authors own all copyrights not held by the publisher.

Legal Notice:

This book is copyright protected. This is only for personal use. You cannot amend, distribute, sell, use, quote or paraphrase any part or the content within this book without the consent of the author or copyright owner. Legal action will be pursued if this is breached.

Disclaimer Notice:

Please note the information contained within this document is for educational and entertainment purposes only. Every attempt has been made to provide accurate, up to date and reliable complete information. No warranties of any kind are expressed or implied. Readers acknowledge that the author is not engaging in the rendering of legal, financial, medical or professional advice.

By reading this document, the reader agrees that under no circumstances are we responsible for any losses, direct or indirect, which are incurred as a result of the use of information contained within this document, including, but not limited to, —errors, omissions, or inaccuracies.

Table of Contents

Introduction 7
Chapter One What Are Penny Stocks? 19
Chapter Two Preparing For Penny Stocks 33
Chapter Three How And Where To Purchase 47
Chapter Four Trading Penny Stocks 61
Chapter Five Tracking Your Penny Stocks.................................. 73
Chapter Six Understanding Risk 87
Chapter Seven Having A Solid And Diversified Portfolio 99
Conclusion.. 113

INTRODUCTION

First, we would like to extend our thanks for your purchase of ***Jump Start Your Road To Riches--Maximize Your Profits With Penny Stock Trading***. We hope you will find this book to be informative and a vital part of your road to investments. Congratulations on deciding to take hold of your future and begin investing your money into Penny Stocks as a way to maximize your savings and begin your journey towards your future goals. Making a commitment to savings and investments is an excellent choice and will help you in the future whether you are looking to be financially independent or retire at an early age. Though, the stories of getting rich quickly from Penny Stocks are far and few, this type of investment is an excellent way to diversify your portfolio and invest in lower risk types of financial planning.

When you are entering the world of investments, the amount of choices that you have can be incredibly daunting and difficult to maneuver your way through. Penny stocks are great ways to dip your toes into playing the stock market but with smaller risks and lower upfront financial requirements. Though these types of assets may be small to medium in risk, no matter what your investment, you always want to find the best tricks and plans to get every penny from your investment. In this book, you will be given the tools and know how that will allow you to maneuver through the Penny stock arena confidently. The tips, tricks, and informative information will also enable you to maximize your returns from your penny stocks which will increase your earning potential, move your goals forward, and diversify your investment portfolio all while giving you excellent preliminary experience in the stock buying and trading industry.

You cannot start any type of investment without a thorough understanding of where your money is going and how exactly the process works. This book will start off by first giving you the ins and outs of what exactly Penny stocks are. We will cover the history of Penny stocks and how they compare to the stocks that you see being traded every minute for hundreds of dollars per share. You will learn the who, what, where, why, and when of Penny stocks which will enable you to responsibly and comfortably dive into the world of the stock exchange but with a risk level that new investors should be comfortable with. Your money is being invested in order to maximize your savings, net worth, and to reach the goals that you have set out for your future so there cannot be silly mistakes made simply because you don't understand the system fully.

There are many ways you can go about investments, but the best tactic is to ease in on your own so that you can learn the ropes before often hiring pricey brokers who will talk with you about certain investments in particular but will not help you understand the process. Even if you choose to hire a representative or agent down the line, it is vital to your future to know how the system works and where exactly your money goes. We will discuss the differences in brokers, representatives and when and why you would need to hire them, and all within the first chapter of this book. Though you may be eager to jump right into Penny stock investment theory, we are going to move into an entirely crucial step in your investment career that should precede any movement of money, the preparation phase.

It should be said and said again that you should never jump into any investment without thorough research and always have a budget and goal plan done before any investments are made. This sounds like it can be time-consuming, but there is no need to run out and hire a financial planner unless you are planning on investing thousands of dollars a month. If that is the case, I doubt you are actually looking into Penny stocks. The information you need to set up a livable and comfortable investment plan will be explained in detail in Chapter two. We have included step by step instructions on doing a budget, financial and investment plan, and setting up your goals in an understandable and realistic way. Never underestimate the power of preparation, especially when it comes to your future and your finances.

Preparation doesn't just mean you are going to be setting up a list of things to do for the future, training counts towards the things you need to do in the present to get to an investable position for the future. Chapter two will also discuss what your current financial status should look like before you start using money that may not be expendable. We will also talk about savings and backup funds that need to be arranged as well as credit cards and any other form of debt that may be better handled before investing begins. Going into your portfolio with a stable financial footing is an excellent way to maximize every dollar you have to invest, even if you are only venturing into Penny stocks. This chapter is vital to the success of long-term investments and reaching the financial goals you set for yourself.

Once you have researched Penny stocks, understood how they function on a daily basis and have prepared your finances to the point to where investments are feasible, it is time to find and purchase your first stock. Due to Penny stock's popularity and the wonderful invention of the internet you can quickly become bogged down with a hundred different sites that are offering

Penny stock purchases. In this chapter, we will begin to review some of the most popular websites for Penny stocks. We will discuss how many locations you should be working with and what you can do to maximize your profits while maintaining a workable system.

After you have decided on a location to make your financial investment, it is vital that you know how to purchase your stocks. With most of these websites, the actual function of purchasing is as easy as a click of a button but the physical part of the purchase is not the only how you need to be aware of. When we speak of penny stocks one of the most important "how's" that you need to understand is how to choose the stock that fits your investments the best. Most likely you will be purchasing several different stocks, but these stocks need to be researched and understood before purchase. We will discuss how to find the perfect stocks that will maximize your return and yield high dividends. Once you have decided on the stocks you will purchase, and you successfully make that investment, it is then time to begin thinking about how to trade these stocks once they are at that point.

You hear about stock trading on a regular basis from the news to the business section of the newspaper but fortunately with Penny stocks the process of trading isn't as in depth as your larger stock exchange investments. You do not need a broker to trade your stocks. However, before we get into the physical act of stock trading, we will first discuss why stocks are sold and how to understand when you have reached the point with your investment to consider a trade. Understanding timing and knowing the signs that will lead you to trade your stocks is paramount and can play a key factor in the maximization of your money but can also, if done incorrectly, can lose you money quickly. The beginning of this section is set up to educate and teach you about trading strategies and timings before you jump into the actual act of trading.

When you have mastered the understanding of when to trade your stocks you are ready to review your investments and decide on a course of action. When that course of action leads to trade you want to be prepared to do so quickly but intelligently. Unfortunately, even in the Penny Stock sector of investments, often stocks change at a blink of an eye and moving quickly can save you money and frustration. Of course, before you trade you always want to understand the company and the stocks you are trading for before jumping into an investment. Just because it seems glamorous on the outside doesn't mean it is worth a trade. You may be tempted, because these investments are little financial contributions, to trade on a whim but if you follow the guidance to trading and choosing stocks you are not only maximizing every penny you put in, you are also preparing yourself for investments in larger stocks that can be risky but yield substantial returns.

Once you have purchased and traded, you want to make sure you are tracking your investments. Tracking can start to consume you, so it is important to limit yourself to at most once a day for tracking. You want to see how your stocks are faring in the market and if they are reaching a peak. It is also good to track assets when there is a natural disaster, a controversy in the company, or new laws that directly affect the area in which your stocks operate. We dive into how to track each one of your stocks and how to efficiently manage them when you are investing in multiple different companies. Organization of your portfolio and your investments is one of the key things that will help you maximize your returns and keep you on the up and up with new and exciting investments.

Risk is involved in every type of investment even down to savings accounts, though their risk is very low. You may consider Penny Stocks as a low-risk investment because you are working with minuscule amounts of money per stock, but a risk is more about the opportunity to lose your investment then it is the worth of your inventory. Penny stocks can often be precarious because you are dealing with smaller companies that are sometimes startups. You want to make sure to manage these stocks with the same careful quality that you would if your stocks were in the hundreds or thousands of dollars and place them in your portfolio under medium to high-risk investments. Never underestimate the earning potential of a company and when you feel that, through research and understanding of the company's financial growth, the stock will continue to grow, there is no requirement that you trade it or cash out. The likelihood of hitting it big from a Penny Stock is small but it does exist, so you want to trust your research and your gut when it comes time to trade your stocks.

Tracking your stocks can be a little intimidating if you don't understand the lingo and charting that the exchange uses to represent your companies. In Chapter Six we will begin the chapter by breaking down the most important parts of the tracking system. This information can be used in any type of stock tracking but is great to perfect when you are investing in Penny Stocks. There are so many different aspects of a stock that you need to familiarize yourself with in order to make smart choices and maximize your return on investment. Once you have mastered the ability to track your stocks comprehensively, you then need to find the right avenue to do so. Watching CNN every day is not a good enough effort in tracking stocks, and there are a plethora of sites online that can help you find your resting place.

In this chapter, we will maneuver out of learning how to translate the information on the screen to real-time data and move into a review of the different sites that you can use to track your investments. You may find that the location you use to trade is the place you are most comfortable tracking your investments but don't stop there. Look into all of the different companies that put out stock data on an hourly basis so that you can pick and choose the places you go for different data. You may find that one site is easier to translate than others, so you don't want to limit yourself to just your home reference point. Use all available tools to help you with your tracking and remember that a lot of the different sites offer assistance and educational tools that will help you really develop your skills in the stock market.

By this point, you have learned what Penny Stocks are, how to prepare yourself for your investment opportunity, how to purchase and trade Penny stocks and ultimately how to track them to maximize your return on investment. The last chapter will focus on life after Penny stocks and how to diversify your portfolio while staying in your comfort zone with risk. As stated earlier Penny stocks are an incredible way to invest small amounts of money, learn the system, and educate yourself on the stock market but they should not be the end of your investment strategy. Diversifying and building your portfolio is crucial in order to protect yourself against loss, make the financial goals you have set out to reach, and ensure yourself a financial freedom that you desire. Portfolio diversification can be done on your own, or you can also invest in financial assistance from a firm or your bank to help you make the smartest decisions for the future of your investments.

The last chapter of this book will really give you some solid information on what diversification really means and how to achieve it in your portfolio. We will discuss why your portfolio is important and how to build that portfolio with different risk levels. There will be a quick but informational section that describes the various levels of risk and examples of what types of investments fall into each category. We will also explain why it is important to incorporate investments that fit your lifestyle while still keeping the quality of life that you are used to. This book will not only give you the tools to maximize your results from Penny Stocks, but it will also enable you to move forward in your financial investments ultimately creating a portfolio that pushes you to meet and exceed all of your future goals on an economic level. Lastly, in this chapter, we will explain how to physically create your portfolio in a way that easily allows you to do a quarterly review of your investments and make changes as your goals and plans for the future move and change.

Beginning your investment adventure or your stock experience with Penny Stocks is an incredibly smart and safe way to ease yourself into the stock market while earning returns on some of the most volatile stocks on the market. You may look at the minuscule cost of these assets and think that this investment is not worth your time, but you have to remember that every company started out somewhere and each investment has the opportunity to blossom into the next Apple, Tesla, or General Motors. One important thing to remember is that not every stock will be a winner, and you may even lose money on some of them, but that is the love-hate relationship with the stock market; when you end up choosing the right investment you will be left with a sense of accomplishment, love for the profession, and a sizeable return. Playing it safe is never a bad thing no matter how many movies portray the risk taker as the winner and educating yourself will help you make those intelligent financial decisions.

We would like to thank you again for purchasing ***Jump Start Your Road To Riches--Maximize Your Profits With Penny Stock Trading*** and hope that your future with investing is robust and bright. There is so much information out there on playing the stock market, and you always want to make sure the advice you are being given is sound and right for your personal financial plan. Always question everything and never feel like you are bullied into a decision if your gut is telling you no then make sure you do your research before purchasing any stock, even Penny Stock. When you are attempting to maximize your return with Penny Stocks be sure to start looking at pennies as massive investments because they may make you huge returns if you play the stock market right. If you nonchalantly view Penny Stocks as insignificant because your investments are dollars instead of hundreds of dollars you are more likely not to pay attention to trends and trade stock that you could have made a big return off of. Also remember that when we say big performance we are talking the percentage of what you put into the stock initially, not the actual financial value of the stock. Good luck on your investment adventure and make sure to take notes on anything you believe is pertinent to your next steps into Penny Stocks.

CHAPTER ONE
WHAT ARE PENNY STOCKS?

Welcome to the wonderful and often stressful world of Penny Stocks. Your investment future is of vital importance and beginning your financial future by investing in Penny Stocks will do more than just earn you return on investment, it will educate you on the world of stocks, trades, and portfolio investments. Before you dive into Penny Stocks, however, you first need to understand what they are. In the following Chapter we will discuss what penny stocks are, their history, how they compare to higher priced stocks, the basic who, what, where, when, and why's, and a thorough explanation of the broker/representative/financial advisor relationship and how it can help and hurt you in your investment future. Everything in this chapter is meant to give you a platform base to start from, and you never want to jump into any investment without knowing exactly what it is and how it will work for you.

The actual definition of Penny Stocks has evolved throughout the years. Originally it was defined as any stock that is traded for under a dollar per share. However, the SEC has since changed that definition to include any stock that is sold for under five dollars a share, broadening your choices when working with Penny Stocks. Most of the companies that you will find that are categorized as Penny Stocks do not trade on the major market exchanges, with a few exceptions. The companies you will be looking into for trading purposes will be small businesses with high liquidity and are subject to limited listing with fewer regulatory requirements. These stocks are often very high risk because these companies are often growing and have limited resources. However, with greater risk can come higher return on investment so don't let the fact that most Penny Stocks are high risk deter you from this type of investment.

History

Penny stocks can be used interchangeably with the term micro-cap stocks. Micro-cap stocks are technically considered as such because of the market capitalizations they are capable of, while Penny stocks are considered on the basis of their price. In general, a stock with a capitalization of fifty dollars and three hundred million dollars is a micro cap. Definitions often vary when it comes to penny stocks because while the Securities and Exchange Commission lists penny stocks as any under five dollars, some set the cut-off point at three dollars and others only consider stocks under one dollar penny stocks. Primarily, however, any stock on the pink sheet or over-the-counter bulletin board to be a penny stock. Since definitions change from place to place, it is important to research with your point of purchase what they consider to be penny stocks. Most of the time, however, if you are signing up to trade penny stocks, that is the only type of stock you will be presented with.

What Makes Penny Stocks So High Risk?

We will get into the difference between levels of risk later on in this book, but to explain penny stocks better, it is important to understand the good and the bad. By definition, high risk investments are those that carry a strong chance that you could lose some or all of your investment. Now don't let that immediately scare you away, the opposite and the biggest reason so many people choose high-risk investments is because your rate of return is often exponentially larger than other types of risk investments. Penny stocks fall into the high-risk category for four reasons which are the lack of substantial information available, the fact that there are little to no minimum standards for the company to follow, penny stocks usually belong to new businesses, so there is little background information available, and their liquidity. Let's dive a little bit further into these four factors that make penny stock high risk.

Lack Of Solid Information Available

One of the biggest parts of forming a successful portfolio is having sufficient information to make educated choices on your investments. For penny stocks, information on the company is often tough to find. A company that is listed on pink sheets face subtle requirements and do not have to file with the SEC and therefore are not publicly scrutinized and regulated as the larger stocks that appear on the New York Stock Exchange and the Nasdaq. Often the information that you do find is not produced from credible sources. When you are investing in penny stocks, always research the root from where your information is coming from, and if it is a paid advertiser or broker, then you may want to look into other avenues. Most companies that are traded are available for contact as well so feel free to reach out to them directly, though their information will be inherent bias.

Very Little Background Information Available

It is often discovered that many of the penny stock or micro-cap stocks have either just formed as a company or are nearing bankruptcy. When a company is brand new there is inherently no background information for them to give so you will have little to go off of. When a corporation is nearing bankruptcy, they either have not done a good job keeping historical records or they keep them from the public view. If you are researching a company and have found they have been in business for a while but have little background information you should probably move on to a different company. Remember that not all penny stock companies fall into one of these categories, but it is best to understand the worse case scenario before you start investing money into these unknown businesses. It is very rare that you will find a well-known company in the penny stock arena, so research is essential in this line of investments.

Lack Of Minimum Standards

Standard requirements are way less stringent for stocks on the OTCBB and pink sheets and therefore are less likely to be monitored closely. There is also a chance that this is exactly why a stock is on one of those exchanges. A lot of times when a company is no longer able to meet the requirements of the major exchanges they join the pink sheets or the OTCBB. The OTCBB is slightly more stringent with their rules and requires companies to file their paperwork in a strict timeframe with the SEC. The pink sheets have no such requirement and can often be a haven for businesses that want to stay under the radar but still on the market. The minimum standards we are talking about can be considered a safety net for investors and a goal or bragging right for the company. Knowing your investment in stock is protected by at least the minimum standards a company should adhere to can help you feel more comfortable when investing your money.

Liquidity

Liquidity in the stock market is defined as the amount of action the stock is receiving during a particular period. When a stock doesn't have a high liquidity in can become tough to sell that stock. If the level of liquidity is considered small, you may be able to find a buyer, but you will most likely be required to lower the price of the stock in order to attract those customers. A low liquidity can also lend to fraud or manipulation of the share prices. The easiest way to manipulate these stocks is by buying massive amounts of stock, get people excited about it, and then sell it after other investors start to become interested. This manipulation is usually done by the company or by someone very familiar with the stock industry and is known as pump and dump in the investment world. Make sure always to do your due diligence when it comes to investments and don't listen to the hype by random investors or companies.

Common Scams To Watch Out For

With the minimum standards that penny stock companies need to reach and the lack of knowledge and background information on these businesses, penny stocks can fall victim to scams pretty quickly. The SEC regards these types of stocks a pain in their butts, but they continue to allow the investment community to take part since it can be incredibly lucrative when done the correct way. There are many different scams out there, but the two most used are the recommendations based on biased backgrounds and the brokers offshore. Again, these are not anywhere near the only two scams that are circulating the penny stock industry, but these are definitely two of the most famous and the most important for you to be aware of. Let's take a closer look at both types of scams and how to avoid them.

Biased Recommendations

There are some companies out there that will pay people or businesses to recommend their stock to you. These recommendations will come in many different ways including newsletters, radio, and commercial television. Even your email will not be safe from this biased salesman and you could receive spam that is attempting to entice you into purchasing specific stocks. You should never take any of these false promotions seriously, and you should also stay away from those particular investments. A dead giveaway that you are being made victim to this scam is a disclaimer providing the information that the advertiser is being paid by someone to represent this investment stock. Press releases are also ways that these stocks can be promoted, so you want to make sure you find out the legitimacy of any press release you read before taking its advice and purchasing the stock.

Brokers Offshore

Regulations by the SEC allow companies to sell stock outside of the United States to investors and are exempt from registering that stock. Companies will sell the stock to foreign brokers at a discounted rate. The brokers then, after purchasing the stock, turn around and sell it back to U.S. investors for a huge profit. These agents use high-pressure tactics to sell this stock such as cold calling investors that have substantial financial availability to purchase the stock and give misleading but attractive information about the assets in order to get the investors to buy the stock. These brokers also employ very harsh sales tactics when attempting to sell their shares which are not the typical action of an investment broker. To be safe stay away from all foreign agents and choose to work with brokers that work for reputable and well-known firms if you decide to go that route. Anyone cold-calling for investments is not usually someone you want to trust with your financial future.

Broker/Financial Planner Relationship

When you are entering the financial investment arena, you will be faced with the decision to employ an investment broker and/or a financial advisor. These two people do different things but can be useful in specific situations. All in all, however, penny stocks are not really the types of investments you will want to employ a broker or advisor for since their cost could quickly eat up your profit. Regardless of that, it is vital for you to understand both of these positions and how they can work for you as you continue to diversify your portfolio and possibly enter into the larger stock arena. Advisors can also be useful resources when attempting to do research on specific stocks or investments. We are going to take a look at both the investment broker and the financial advisor and the duties of both of them.

Broker

An investment broker is a person that brings companies selling stock together with an investor looking to purchase stock. Investment brokers are usually required to be licensed and can work for both the seller and the buyer in the stock management arena. Generally, the agent only acts on behalf of the client and follows their instructions. Agents are paid through fees charged for services which can range in price depending on the firm, the job, and the stock that is being worked with. Three of the main ways that brokers make their money is through commissions, margin interest charges, and fees for service. Beyond handling the stocks for clients, brokers are often also allowed to provide investment advice and offer limited banking services such as check writing and opening interest bearing savings accounts, but they primarily work strictly with selling and buying stocks for their clients. The main thing you need to know is that you will sometimes have to work with brokers and when it is not demanded you need to know when it will be helpful.

Brokers aren't going to give you the ins and outs of increasing your portfolio and their service fees for investment advice can sometimes be absolutely astronomical. You want to remember that, though we hope the people handling our money have integrity, brokers work for both the company and the investor so taking investment advice can sometimes be biased. When you really need to decide on hiring or using brokerage services is when you are planning to purchase larger or restricted stocks in the major markets. Some of the stocks on the main markets are required to use a broker to go between the company and the investor and are not publicly sold. You can get a broker by using the brokers at the company in which you trade through, or you can hire a broker from a local firm. The brokers working for the larger financial firms usually have their finger on the pulse of the investment world and often charge way less of a fee than hiring someone privately to handle your purchases. Either way, brokers are not necessary for penny stocks nor do many of them offer their services in that field.

Financial Advisor

Technically financial advisors can be considered brokers, lawyers, planners, etc. so for this book we are going to talk about planners. Financial planners are professionals that assist their clients in setting up a plan for their financial investments and portfolios. You can find financial planners at firms and also through your bank. The charges that you may incur from a financial planner depend on your level of services and what financial investments you choose to participate in through this professional. The important part of a planner is to get you into a financial position to engage in the investment world and create a diversified portfolio. Most investments made through a financial planner are your lower risk investments such as IRA's, bonds, and high-interest bank accounts. Most financial planners are not brokers, but many brokers are also financial planners though their loyalties are often in conflict due to their buyer/seller relationships.

Financial planning can be extremely expensive, but there comes the point in almost every person's financial investment plan that a planner is necessary. One superb reason to hire a planner would be when you reach a period in your financial future that you are unsure of what the next step should be. When you hit these walls with your financial investment future, it is important to hire someone that can lead you in the right direction. Another good reason to hire a professional is when you look at money and financial planning, and you just have no interest in handling it yourself. These moments can easily lead to no or little planning which can be detrimental to your financial future so make sure to go to the professional if this is just not your cup of tea. Also, if you are taking a self-promote position in handling your own finances, you may want to hire a planner in order to be an impartial person to review your plan. By using a planner for a review, you are assuring yourself the best plan possible since they will be able to offer better or more lucrative solutions to your investment and portfolio project.

Whether you are looking to bring a professional into your project or just looking to the future, the information in this chapter has given you a solid understanding of the investment world. Penny stocks may have risks and may not be something you want to sink all of your money into, but they can result in very lucrative investment returns if you choose to follow the guidelines and safety rules that we have expressed so far in this book. Making financial choices is paramount but can be very nerve racking without the proper education. Creating a diverse portfolio is imperative to reaching your financial goals for the future and penny stocks are definitely an amazing way to give your portfolio that diversification. Penny stocks are also great learning tools for when you decide to move into larger more expensive stocks but remember that they are way less restrictive and usually a bit higher risk than those stocks on the major exchanges. Do your research, decide intelligently on assistance through brokers and planners, and you have no choice but to be successful in your endeavors with penny stocks and micro-cap investments. Now that you understand penny stocks it is now time to begin preparing for your investment future.

CHAPTER TWO
PREPARING FOR PENNY STOCKS

By following the directives in this chapter, you will not only be prepared to start your penny stock investment, but you will be ready for your entire portfolio journey. Financial investments are imperative to the success of your future but you never just want to rush in without preparing your life and finances for a change. The first project you need to do before starting any financial plan is to steady your current finances. We will start this chapter with a discussion on the initial commercial preparation you must start with before beginning your investing. We will then talk about goal setting and how that affects your entire portfolio. Once we have made it through your goal setting and we have a firm idea of what your future goals need to become a reality, we will tackle creating a financial assessment and plan. All of these things will lead you to the ultimate point where you can begin trading in penny stocks.

Initial Financial Preparation

Before you even start thinking about your goals and plans, you need to get your current financial situation into a perfect standing and responsible rhythm. Though you may not be able to pay off every loan you have, especially loans like a house, car, or student loan, you will want to minimize your monthly spending to a comfortable level. We will discuss investing according to your lifestyle later in this chapter but for now make sure when you are reducing your expenses and preparing for investment you are doing it in a way that you still have an active quality of life in the now or that could lead to financial issues and even departure from your future financial plans. There is no need to live by candlelight for ten years just to get to your goals, and it is not recommended to cut out everything in the now to reach to reach the future, though you may want to sacrifice certain things like not eating out as much and curbing your shopping habits.

Probably the most important financial stepping stone is to take a look at your emergency fund if you even have one at all. You need to have an emergency fund with a minimum of one year worth of bills in it, and a year is recommended. In order to do this, you want to write down all of your bills that are not going to change such as an average utility, mortgage or rent, cell phone bill, student loan payment, car payment, insurance, etc. Then you want to take that total number and multiply it by six or twelve, and you will get the total you need to have in a savings account in case of emergency, loss of job, or illness. You never want to put this money in an account that is going to be hard to access or invoke penalties for withdrawing money from it. Though you don't want to touch these funds unless necessary, you also want to be able to get to it quickly in case of emergency.

Another aspect of getting your finances in order will include deciding what loans you are able to pay off and which ones are there no matter what. If you have acquired credit card debt, then you need to pay off their balances before you start throwing money into other ventures. When you have a balance on a credit card, you are literally throwing money away to interest; money you could be using to invest in your future. Credit cards don't have to be considered a negative thing, but you want to limit your spending on it and pay it off as quickly as you can in order to be in as little debt as possible. As far as student loans go you want to find out if you are paying the minimum you can get away with. You don't want to agree on a huge number just to get them paid off and end up putting yourself in a bad position if money becomes an obstacle and you are always able to add more to a monthly payment if you want to, but keep it at a small pay for now. Other loans such as car and house may be something that you can't pay off completely so just get into a solid rhythm with those payments and accept they are there for the long haul.

As far as getting your finances in order the last thing you should look at is how you could comfortably minimize your bills while still allowing for a high quality of life. This action is not meaning to look at all of your extra expenditures, that will be tackled later in the planning stage, this is more looking at your monthly bills and seeing what could be gotten rid of or reduced. For example, if you work a fifty hour a week job, go to yoga three times a week, and only turn the television on Saturday night you might want to consider Netflix instead of a hundred dollar cable plan that you never actually use. Representatives at your bank can be contacted and asked about refinancing your mortgage which may result in a lower interest, lower payments, and a lower final payout in the end. There are a lot of things you can do to cut dollars here and there but don't go crazy with things like utilities; it is unrealistic to think you can live without heat in Alaska for a year.

Goal Setting

Without a firm set of goals, how would you keep track of what you are investing and planning for in the future? If you do not know what you are planning for you will have no idea how to structure your investment strategy. Goals are important in every aspect of life, and that is no different when you are financially planning for the future. It is important to have both short and long term goals in mind in order to keep yourself accountable and motivated with your investment portfolio. A short-term goal may be a vacation, an early payoff on your mortgage, or even a career change. A long-term goal may be financial freedom or retirement strategy. Whatever your goals are you want to organize them and get them down on paper so you can keep track and adjust your investments as you get further into your financial management. One of the most important things to remember is that you want to be reasonable with your goals so that you don't make risky investments to push quickly to a target that you may not reach in the time you have allotted. We all would like to make a million dollars in a year with investments, but that is not a reasonable goal unless you are starting with that much to invest.

Deciding on manageable and realistic goals can be a challenge when you are looking at the opportunity to make some of your future dreams come true, but you need to stay grounded. The more stress you put on reaching these goals, the more likely you are to make risky investment decisions which could ultimately cost you a lot of money and a lot of time. When you create the goal sheet in this chapter, you want to really look at what kind of financial investment will be needed to make this goal a reality and give yourself a reasonable amount of time to reach it. We suggest adding at least one year to your estimated time period in order to give yourself ample opportunity to focus on more than just one of your goals at a time. Always create a system that challenges you but doesn't overwhelm so that you are more inept to continue your financial plan even when things don't go quite as you had measured them to. Let's take a look at a template for creating and organizing your goals.

Short or Long Term Goal Planning Template

List Of Short Term Goals

    1.

    2.

    3.

I.   Goal One Title

- Goal 1 Timeline:
- Goal 1 Cost Analysis:

    Section Costs:

    Total Cost:

- Goal 1 Total Financial Requirements: $

II. Goal Two Title

- Goal 2 Timeline:
- Goal 2 Cost Analysis:

    Section Costs:

    Total Cost:

- Goal 2 Total Financial Requirements: $

III. Goal Three Title

- Goal 3 Timeline:
- Goal 3 Cost Analysis:

    Section Costs:

    Total Cost:

- Goal 3 Total Financial Requirements: $

For the short term goal sheet you want to start by listing one to three pertinent short term goals. Be sure not to overload yourself with short term goals and remember once one is reached you can always add more. You want to title each goal and then go through the steps in order to break them down. The timeline is going to be how long you want it to take or how long you have to achieve that goal. The cost analysis will take a little more work because you don't want just to put a total cost. Breaking down the financial requirements to reach that goal will help you understand and research that goal. You may find a cheaper but equally efficient avenue to achieving your goal which can help you meet deadlines. Lastly, for each goal, you want to total it up and have a firm total of what you will need to complete this aim. Long term goals are relatively the same, but you will have to put a lot more time into the cost analysis of each one and I recommend no more than two lofty long-term goals.

Creating goals that are reasonable and achievable are crucial. Your goals can and should push the envelope, but they also need to be something you can actually achieve based on your personal position and finances. Setting goals that put too much pressure on your investments can cause several negative responses. When you are feeling pressed to reach a financial goal you may haphazardly place investments unwisely in order to make the most money the fastest. Unfortunately, when you make investments without due diligence, you are setting yourself up to not only lose a profit but to lose the entire amount of money you invested initially, which will only set you back in your timeline. Also, when goals are set that are not achievable you will have the want to quit or lose interest in your financial future, and that is not a way to reach goals. We need short term goals in order to push ourselves for the long term ones which tend to be the financially larger goals.

Financial Assessment

Your financial assessment is a way, not only to see where each part of your money goes but to figure out how much expendable cash you have to invest. You can also find interesting trends in your spending habits when you do a financial assessment. Though you can sit down and do an investment in a day using your memory and billing statements, my suggestion is to take one entire month and go through your month like usual, taking a receipt for everything you do. Put all of those receipts into an envelope, or many envelopes if you are organized, and keep them for the next month. Then, when you have gone through a typical month, you will sit down and go through everything you spent money on during that last month, inputting it into a financial assessment spreadsheet. Now, you can get as specific or as general as you'd like but to really understand where your money is going, how you can cut back, and how much you have to spend on investments, the more accurate, the better. Here is an example of a middle of the pack type of financial assessment that you can use.

Financial Assessment

Housing Expenses
Net Monthly Income

Rent/Mortgage: $_____   Take Home Wage 1: $_____

    2nd Mortgage: $_____   Take Home Wage 2: $_____

    Property Taxes: $_____   Other Income: $_____

    Insurance: $_____   Total Income: $_____

    Basic Utilities: $_____

    Assoc. Dues: $_____

    Sub-Total: $_____

Living Expenses Monthly   ### Leftover

Food: $_____   Income Total: $_____

Clothing: $_____   <u>Monthly Expense Total</u>: $_____

Transportation: $_____ Cash Flow Total: $_____

Insurance: $_____ (subtract Monthly ET from Income)

Daycare: $_____

Medical Expense: $_____

Sub-Total: $_____

Other Monthly Debt

Car Payment: $_____

Child Support/Alimony: $_____

Credit Card Payment: $_____

Credit Card Payment: $_____

Credit Card Payment: $_____

Other: $_____

Sub-Total: $_____

Monthly Expenses

(Add All Expense Subtotals Together)

Total: $_____

Your total cash flow will be what you should have left over at the end of every month after all of your bills. That being said, if you do this sheet and find that the number you should have left over does not equal what you actually have leftover it is now time to look at all the receipts of extra expenditures and see where the rest of your money is going. Understanding where you spend your expendable cash flow will help you understand your quality of life as well as where you feel comfortable cutting back in order to better reach your goals. Do not take the cash flow total and plan to invest it all unless you are going to travel to work every day, go home, and never do anything social. Always allow yourself enough space to live within your means but to enjoy life a little while you are preparing for the future. Now you need to take this assessment and all the above information and plug it into your financial plan for your investments.

Personal Investment Plan

Your personal investment plan is a culmination of all of the preparation work you just completed. This plan is going to take the numbers you need for your goals, your available investable funds, and your investment ideas and put them into a workable and realistic goal. Now it would be great if it was magic and did it on its own, but unfortunately, this is going to take some research and math unless you decide to hire a financial planner to do it for you. One of the initial steps that you want to take when completing your investment plan is to decide upon your risk profile, meaning what do is the most risk you need to take to reach your goals in the allotted timeframe. You may find out you don't need to invest heavily in high-risk investments and instead can work with penny stocks and then an array of low to medium risk strategies. After you decided on this, you want to decide how you want to split your diversification in your portfolio remembering that you don't want to put all of your money into one basket.

Investment plans are incredibly in-depth processes and take up a lot of time, so it is not viable to place a template in this book. However, there are many free resources on the web that can guide you through the process. Some of the information that you see may seem like it is repetitive or not necessary but trust us, when it all culminates together you will have a clear picture of what your investment future holds. When it comes to penny stocks you understand that you are placing investments in a high-risk strategy but if you play the market safely, you will be getting excellent returns on investment and diversifying your portfolio with each new investment. Some of the lower risk investments may seem perfect for the part of your portfolio but may require a substantial investment and penny stocks are a great way of reaching those minimums and reinvesting your money.

You're Ready To Move Into Your Penny Stock Investment

Once you have done all of the preparation work and have a solid financial investment plan to reach your stated goals, it is now time to move into the actual investment parts. You have made it through the most labor-intensive part of the process but having this concrete example of your financial status, your financial future, and your strategy will allow you guide yourself through the investment process. Understanding these things will also help you when your goals shift or change along the way. Remember, if your goals change you need to take a new look at your investment plan and adjust the plan accordingly. It is recommended to review your portfolio and investment plan each year but quarterly would give you the opportunity to better have a handle on your finances and allocation of funds. In today's society, our lives change so quickly, and you want to make sure you are adjusting your portfolio accordingly so that you don't run into a tight spot.

CHAPTER THREE
HOW AND WHERE TO PURCHASE

Congratulations on getting your financial affairs in order, planning your future goals, and setting an investment strategy of success. I know you are probably anxious to start trading even if this isn't your first foray into the stock exchange system. Understanding your different options for trading penny stocks is crucial, and you always want to do business with a reputable and trustworthy company. Since penny stocks are such high risk and are left open to so many different scams, it is recommended that you do your trading through a brokerage firm. Often times these companies can give you top information on the companies you are investing in and can also lead you to higher stocks in the future. However, don't feel that just because you signed onto a particular firm that you have to use all of their services, they are there to make money too, and sometimes these companies offer services you don't really need for a high cost. One of the main things to attempt to do when trading with penny stocks is minimized your cost and maximize your revenue.

Now that you are ready to dive into your investment it is important to understand three main areas of penny stocks. In this chapter, we will discuss how to purchase penny stocks, how to maximize your revenue from penny stocks, and we will compare multiple different companies so that you can decide who is the best choice for your investment needs. Make sure that you are also doing some other type of investment during this period, preferably in your low-risk category so that you can be maximizing your investments and protecting yourself if you run into a bad purchase in your penny stock trade. Trading penny stocks will become second nature to you after you understands the ins and outs of the business. Let's start things off by discussing how exactly you purchase penny stocks.

How To Purchase Penny Stocks

Let's be honest you don't need a broker to buy penny stocks; you can buy penny stocks through online websites on your own. The money you are investing and returning doesn't warrant paying a broker ridiculous amounts of money to do something you can do yourself. Even on these sites, you will be approached by agents, though most of them tend to stick to stocks sold on the major exchanges. If you have questions about what you are doing, most of the websites have free help, forums, or chatting availability. Also, don't underestimate the power of the internet where you can find answers to literally everything. When you sign up for a site, put the money into your account that you plan on trading with and are sitting in front of the computer looking at an absorbent amount of data you need to follow some clear steps to purchase the right penny stock.

Step One- Research

I know, you are probably deathly tired of hearing the word research, but it really is the only way to understand what you are getting ready to purchase. As we have said before it may be difficult to find a lot on these companies because they are often new but it is important to investigate the financial history of any company you plan on investing in. Google Finance and Yahoo Finance are excellent places to find information on small to medium sized companies. When you are researching stocks that are specifically pinned to the OTC penny stock market, you can find really helpful information with services like the OTC Bulletin Board and the National Quotation Bureau. One of the best stocks to consider are IPO's which are Initial Public Offerings and come from companies newly entering the market. However, make sure to read all the information about the business before putting in a bid in order to ensure you are making a wise decision.

Step Two-Look Out For Fraud

I know we covered fraud in the last chapter, but it is so important that it needed to be added to the steps to purchasing stock. Penny stocks, unfortunately, can be overrun by fraudulent assets and deals, so you need to have your spidey sense going when you are looking into specific areas of investments. In the last chapter, we discussed "pump and dump" where an investor buys a lot of stock for a low price and then sells it an increased cost to other investors. This dishonest tactic can leave you with a high purchase price even though the company value has not changed. The main way to avoid these situations is never to listen to the advice you haven't sought from a professional in the industry. "Hot" stocks through phone calls, emails, and other sources is a blaring sign that this stock is in fact not worth much at all and you could be left with nothing in the end. Always be aware and stay vigilant.

Step Three- Open Your Account

The next step is the most exciting part of the process, and that is opening your account with an online brokerage firm. We will go over some of the most popular websites later in this chapter but start thinking sites like E-Trade and TD Ameritrade. These sites allow you to deposit a small amount into a secured account that you will be using to purchase stock, pay fees, and collect revenue from the sale of shares. These sites also give you vital information on the stock market, current trends, and volatility of the different penny stocks. Make sure you pick a reliable and well-known site to start your penny stock trading. There is no need to have several different locations to purchase from since the stock will be the same price on every site, the difference in cost will be the fees that are charged by the broker.

Step Four-Begin Purchasing And Trading

Once you have done all of the above, researched, and chosen the stocks you are going to start investing in then it is time to start bidding and purchasing shares. You want always to limit your purchase instead of using market orders since limit orders award you the ability to control the price of the transaction. Market orders are utilized in the larger stock areas but with penny stocks you may find you are losing money since people often bid too high initially on these investments. Also, make sure to look through the website since they usually provide step by step instructionals on the best-used practices for penny stocks.

How To Maximize Your Returns

The entire point of these types of investments is to get as much return as possible on the stocks that you purchase. Maximizing your returns does not just mean picking the perfect stock and selling at the right time, there are many other ways that you can get the most from your stock purchases. In order to reach your selected goals, you need to make the most out of every penny you have. Not everyone playing the penny stock market is limited to that because of finances, and that should tell you there is sufficient money to be made if you follow the right path. As with anything you buy in life you want to get the most for your money and in the stock industry that is ROI's or returns on investment. For this book, we are going to look at four relevant and informative ways to not only maximize your return on investment but also avoid massive losses. Short term trading, the stop loss tool, moderate training, and understanding your companies are the four most vital things that you can do to maximize and avoid loss when trading penny stocks.

Short-Term Trading

There are two distinct ways that you can manage your stocks, short-term or long-term investing. Long-term investments are what happens when you purchase stock and then sit on it for extended periods of time, decades even, and ride out the ups and downs of the stock market. This type of strategy is good for your larger publicly traded stocks because they have more stringent guidelines than penny stocks do. The short-term investment would literally be purchasing a stock and then selling it as soon as you've made some money from it. You can either go with your gut or give yourself a time frame and a dollar amount that you want to see from the trade but in order for that to work you have to stick to the plan. It is very easy to make money off of a stock and get greedy, deciding to hold out a little bit longer, which can often cause you to lose your gains. It is kind of like playing the slots at a casino; you may get half way through your night and be up by 100%, and instead of cashing in and taking the win you continue on your "hot streak" and end up leaving with less than what you came with.

The Stop Loss Tool

The stop loss tool is so valuable, yet people often forget to use it. Not every stock you buy will make you money, and in fact, you may lose money on some of them. Part of the capital industry investment strategy is to let it fluctuate and hopefully be able to see it when you have reached the desired return, but sometimes when it goes down, it continues to go down. However, let's face it, most people investing in penny stocks don't have the time to day trade and can purchase a stock at lunch, go back hours later and find their account severely detrimental. This is where the stop loss feature comes into play. You are able to set a maximum loss for a stock or group of stocks so that you do not face massive losses. A stop loss will end the trade when it reaches a certain loss or alert you that you are getting close so that you can go in and make your next choice in moves.

Trade Moderately And Intelligently

Regardless of all of the warnings we have given so far in this book, there are a lot of good, reliable companies in the penny stock arena. Don't focus on taking so many chances; penny stocks are already high risk. Instead, look for the businesses that are stable with smart products and a good restructuring plan. Many times companies that are going into bankruptcy are the companies to invest in because they are going to start fresh with a new plan of attack. Make sure when you are looking at those types of businesses you are pinpointing the reason for bankruptcy and find out how their product popularity was before the company took a turn towards bankruptcy. In today's economic climate it is not strange to see companies with bankruptcy begin to rise strongly again as the economy grows, many people took a hit when the economy crashed.

Know Your Companies!

We cannot drag this point home enough; you need to know as much about your companies as you possibly can in order to make smart choices with your investments. There are many diverse businesses in the stock exchange and technology runs rampant through them, but you don't want to invest in a company that supplies a product or service that you don't know anything about. If you are inexperienced or not knowledgeable about what the company does then how can you decide if what they do is a viable business option that would warrant your investment? You wouldn't want to invest in a company that created solar systems if you don't know anything about them, the market, or the need for them in the general populace. Stick with what you know and you will see a lot higher return on investment since your expertise will lend a hand in choosing bid price and when to sell.

Different Online Brokerages

Selecting an online brokerage site to work with can be just as important as choosing the stocks you are going to be investing. You want a company that is going to provide you some information, track the stocks accurately, and have low to no fees to trade penny stocks. You also want a company that has a clean record in the industry since you don't want to add to the risk of your investment by choosing a brokerage firm that has had run-ins with the SEC before. There are so many sites out there now that offer penny stock trading that finding the one that is right for you and your portfolio may be incredibly daunting and confusing. They like to throw a ton of terms at you that may not even go with what you are planning to do in order to cover up some of the higher fees you could be hit with. Due diligence is vital when picking a site. Here are some of the top online brokerage firms for trading penny stocks.

Things To Look For

Before we name off these companies it is important to understand that like the stocks you are getting ready to purchase; the company can sometimes have hidden agendas and fees as well. Not every firm is created equal, and it is sadly up to you to find those minute differences that could make huge differences in your returns. There are three main things that you want to make sure to look for when you are researching online brokerage firms, trade surcharges, volume restrictions, and trade restrictions.

Business surcharges are charges added to stocks based on them being below a certain dollar amount. Most of the time you will be selling penny stocks in large quantities, so you want to make sure the surcharge is a flat fee and not a per share charge. Since everyone has a different definition of what a penny stock is you want to find out the specifics of the site you are working at so that you can base your financial investment around that. Remember, you want to maximize your return which also means getting the least amount of extra fees per transaction as possible.

Volume restrictions are a pain in the butt and are put into place to scrape every bit of commission out of the investor. The best brokers will have no limit on transactions, but a lot of them either charge more for higher volume transactions or restrict the amount of shares you can trade in one day. This limit will cause you to have to come back the next day and pay another commission fee to continue your strategy. Make sure you know what the terms are so that you can make the most out of your trading strategy as possible.

Trade restrictions are something to look out for and ultimately should help you decide on the best site for your penny stock investments. The best sites should allow you to trade penny stocks online just like any other stock out there. However, some firms require you to buy by phone and put limits on the types of deals that you can execute. This tactic allows them to bypass stocks they won't make a high commission on but also blocks you from investing the way you want.

Best Sites

Company	Overview	Commission	Account Minimum	Special Promotions
E-Trade	High Selection with frequent trader offers	$9.99 per trade, volume discount	$500	Sixty Days Of Commission Free Trades With A $10,000 Deposit

Optionsxpress	High selection with free OTC trades	$8.95 per trade	$0	Fifty Commission Free Trades With A $5,000 Deposit
TD Ameritrade	Multi-level trading platforms	$9.99 per trade	$0	Bonus Cash For Large Deposits
Charles Schwab	Multi-level trading platform	$8.95 per trade	$1,000	Bonus Cash For Large Deposits
Merrill Edge	Flat commissions	$6.95 per trade	$25,000	Bonus Cash For Large Deposits
Choice Trade	Flat commissions	$7.00 per OTC trade	$0	None

Whichever company you choose to trade with you want to make sure it fits your goals and your trading strategy. Most of the online trading sites have live chat features that will allow you to ask company specific questions before signing up for an account. The minimum starting balance may be attractive but if you plan on having a larger amount to trade with, some of the higher balance accounts come with perks that you may find helpful.

There is also a plethora of information on these sites on the internet, including reviews by prior and standing investors.

All in all this chapter has covered everything from penny stock best practices to how to pick your online brokerage firm. By this point, you should be settled into your new home and be ready to start making your returns and building your way towards your short and long term goals. Also remember that these online brokerage firms are often multifaceted and can lend a hand when you decide to move into the larger traded stocks on other exchanges.

CHAPTER FOUR
TRADING PENNY STOCKS

We have given you some really appropriate tools and information so far in this book that will lead you to your daily or weekly trading routine. Buying penny stocks is great, but they will do you no good monetarily if you don't trade them and maximize your return on investment. Trading is just as strategic as picking the stocks that you want to purchase and it all kind of melds together into a fluid process where you are trading and buying like a machine. The penny stock industry is definitely something you will have to pay close attention to and though you may not be able to be online all of the time, it is important to check your stocks several times a day and set up alerts that will assist you in catching stocks at their maximum potential for return. Investing in your future is usually something you do while also going about your normal life with work, family, and routine so adding some time in for your trades will be essential for success.

We are not going to get into giving you a step by step process of how to physically sell your stocks. Between the brokerage service you have chosen and the tips and information we have given so far, the technical process should come relatively quickly to you. What does need some attention are the things that you need to remember when you are going through the process of trading. In this chapter, we are going to dive into the best practices for trading your penny stocks. Some of the information may seem repetitive, but that means it is a vital part of the entire process and should be remembered at each turn in your investment strategy. From reading your stocks to selling your shares at the precise moment for maximum returns, let's take a look at the ten most important best practices to successful penny stock management and trading.

One-Success Stories

No matter where you look when you Google penny stocks you are going to find a million stories of success where people turned a thousand dollars into a million dollars. Some of these stories will be articles while others will be those ridiculous schemes asking you to buy their book or hire them to show you how to do the same. No matter what the angle of the success story, ignore it. Don't sign up for extra info, don't be impressed by shiny numbers and short time periods, and don't believe everything you see; this guy may have five students who reached a million dollars in three years but what he doesn't tell you is he has seven hundred thousand students.

Like so many other things in life, there is no magical formula to get you from rags to riches in thirty days. The best thing for you to do is to put your nose to the grind, follow the rules, use your best practices, and focus on your goals. It feels superb when selling your first stock for a positive return but don't run away with that feeling. Instead, use it to see what you did right and wrong and tweak your practice so that the next intelligent purchase you make will yield even higher returns on investment. This investment is for you and your specific goals and if one of them is to make a million dollars you might want to ensure your portfolio is highly diversified because you are not going to find that quick million in penny stocks.

Two-Tips and Disclaimers

When you start buying and selling penny stocks, you are going to find newsletters and emails popping up all over the place. Do not be fooled by the "tips" in these publications; no one gives the info up for free. The SEC requires a company to put a disclosure at the end of an article or promotion if they are being compensated in any way by the parent company of the stock they are promoting. Make sure to check all of the promotions for that disclosure and ignore that information; it's no different than buying shoes from a chain store because the ad says they are the best.

A lot of times you will see stocks reach their 52-week peak, not because the company is doing so well, but because several publications picked up the ad the company paid to place. These tips are useless and can lead you to purchase stock that will crash shortly thereafter and yield you little to negative return on investment. As with anything else, do your research about a company before you purchase and trade. Always ignore the publicized tips and disclaimers about buying specific stock.

Three-Speed Of Sale

One of the biggest mistakes you can make is expecting a thousand percent return on a penny stock. If you wait for that kind of performance, I can promise you will lose more money than you make. A safe and healthy return on a stock is twenty to thirty percent within a few days. This level of return is what makes penny stocks so popular in the investment arena, a relatively stable return in a really short amount of time. Ultimately you are buying in bulk and selling quickly so you may only be making pennies to small dollars on each stock, you are doing that in bulk, in a quick time period, and with little to no work.

This quick turn around on penny stocks is what enables you to make a substantial weekly return on investment because the turnaround time for profit is so short. However, watch out for that devil on your shoulder whispering to stay just a little longer because even if you notice later that stock continued to climb, you saved yourself in the long run because most will top out on returns at that thirty percent mark. Penny stocks are already high risk, don't add to that risk with your behavior in trading.

Four-Company Management

The companies offering the stock will often have many different, but all outstanding, things to say about their business and its future. Just like the promotions you can not believe anything these management members have to say. Would you buy a car from the guy who owns the car company just because he says it's the best car on the market? No, probably not. These companies will say and do anything they can to get you to purchase their stock, and some of the companies are not actually real companies. Many people will create a "company," sell stock and reap the rewards of the return on a company that only exists on paper.

One of the most important points that you need to remember is that no matter what line of stocks you are trading, there are always people trying to rip you off. With penny stocks, the stakes are higher because the regulations are lower when it comes to what is expected through the SEC. Don't believe something until you have gotten the information from a reputable source. If it seems to good to be true, it probably is. Do your research, understand the company, and if in doubt either pass on the stock or go to a professional who will be able to lead you better in the direction you should follow.

Five-Short Selling

A short sale is kind of an opposite way of thinking about stocks. When you purchase a stock, you are hoping its value will rise so that you can sell that stock and make a profit. For example, you buy one share of X Company stock at $100 and the next week the share is worth $150; you could technically sell that stock and make a fifty percent return on investment. Short selling is when an investor borrows a stock has it sold and then hopes the price on the stock goes down so that they can buy it back and make the profit.

For example; Joe borrows ten shares worth $50 and sells them. The 500 dollars is put into his account, and he waits. If the stock goes up to $75 within a week, he will have to buy the shares back, but he will lose money. If the shares go down to $25 he has to buy the shares but he will have made a fifty percent return. There are a lot of rules on the process, but it must go through a broker.

Due to the volatility of penny stocks, it is never a good idea to short sell them. Though some of them might be appealing, you never know if they have been pumped up due to promotion. These two factors make it hazardous to short sell penny stock and the outcomes very rarely outweigh the risk.

Six-Volume

Depending on the brokerage firm, Penny stocks are defined as stocks between less than a dollar and five dollars a share. Due to their low cost you want to buy these stocks in volume in order to maximize your return on investment. Trading penny stocks would be pointless if you were trading one share at a time, making .30 a trade. You are trying to maximize your return and do it within a certain timeframe that you set out when planning your goals and financial assessments. However, be reasonable because if you purchase ten thousand dollars worth on one stock and it plummets you have just lost a lot of money. Find a happy medium between too little and too much when purchasing shares of penny stocks.

When it comes to the volume, you also want to focus that into what stocks you are buying. You want to stay with companies that are selling at least 100,000 shares of stock a day. If you choose stocks with the lower trading volume, you may find yourself in a position where you have a hard time selling that stock off later. If a company's stock has less than 100,000 trades a day and isn't worth more than fifty cents you probably want to leave it alone and move on to something else.

Seven-Stops

Stops were discussed in the last chapter, but there are two ways to look at stops. Most people would say it is smart to utilize your brokerage sites stop loss tool in order to keep yourself from plummeting too far into the negative when a stock doesn't do well. If you are not a person steadily watching the market then you will want to use the stop loss on every purchase you make. However, there is another way to handle this that is slightly riskier and requires self-control and self-interest.

Mental stops are just that; setting your stops based on what you think is best with the stock. You will look at the share and decide what you want to get out of it and then make a mental note of where the cut-off point is. This tactic takes skill and practice in the market, and though risky, can lead to higher rates of return. Mostly you are pushing the boundaries of your stock with no fallback, but your ability to start and stop where you think is best.

Eight-The Best

Without a doubt, you always want to strive to buy the best stock on the market at that given point in time. One of the ways is to track a stock and buy the highest one at its fifty-two-week mark, especially if the stock has seen overall growth. Sometimes this process will take some time, and you will have to track a particular stock for weeks before purchasing it. This dedication is the same as taking the time to research a company before buying its stock. You want to be sure of your investments and treat each and every one as if it is the diamond in the rough that will lead you closer to your goals.

It can be difficult sometimes to watch a stock climb and jump but start to decline when you are ready to purchase, but this is part of the game. You can't always predict what a stock will do, in fact, you can rarely predict what one will do. Sometimes a stock may be doing amazing, but you wake up, and the CEO has passed away with no heir to his thrown, and down the stock prices go. Research and patience, however, can pay off in the long run.

Nine-Large Portions

This essential practice is crucial and is often overlooked. When you purchase penny stocks you are buying in volume but when you sell you don't want to do the same. First of all, you want to limit your stock size regardless of its promise so that you are always able to get out of stock quickly if it begins to decline. When you go to sell the stock, though, regardless of its status you want to space out what you are selling. A good rule of thumb is to never sell more than ten to fifteen percent of the stock's daily volume.

For example, if you bought ten thousand shares of a stock and it is time to sell, you don't want to sell all ten thousand shares at one time. If the daily volume is five thousand, then you want only to sell 500-750 shares of stock a day until it is gone. Of course, if there is an emergency you can sell all of the stock at once but it is safer to sell it in batches then to make significant share sales at once. Some investors may see the large sale as a sign that the stock is not doing well or predicted to do poorly in the upcoming days, making it hard to sell.

Ten-Keep It Professional
Always remember that there is a reason that penny stocks have earned a bad reputation regardless of how well you do at them. Every company will tell you that they have revolutionized the business, that their products will explode, and there aren't any other companies like them in the world. Regardless of your research always stay cynical and careful with your stock purchases. Don't fall in love with a company or a stock even if they stand for everything you do; it is not a smart choice.

You will also find that when you talk to friends and family about your entrance into the penny stock arena, everyone will have an opinion and a suggestion. Though they may be trying to help, make your own choices through solid research and following the guidelines you have set up for yourself. Diversity is incredibly important not just for your overall portfolio but for you penny stock portfolio as well. Stay smart and do what is best for you and your goal tracks and try not to listen to other people and their suggestions.

It is entirely possible to make excellent rates on returns, but you have to be knowledgeable, understand the game, and always have an eye open for scammers who tend to run the penny stock trade. Some investors do not have the kind of capital to purchase shares of Google, so penny stocks are perfect for them. If a stock choice works out then, that person could see huge profits. If you buy a thousand shares of thirty cent stock and that stock goes up to a dollar, you just made four thousand dollars. However, to be smart, you would sell that stock when it reached fifty to seventy-five cents and roll with that return on investment. Yes, you want to maximize your investments, but you want to do it in a safe manner and not hedge bets on companies that may or may not be there when you wake up in the morning. Waiting for a stock to quadruple in the penny stock arena is risky and rarely happens so capitalize on your gains and move forward.

This chapter has given you the ins and outs of the best practices to follow when trading your stocks. These are just initial practices and as time goes on you will be able to add to your list of do's and dont's that work for you with penny stocks. The common theme in penny stock trading is using your head and researching everything. You also must always be aware that there are people and companies out there looking to cheat you out of your investments which can ultimately set you back in your goals. Now that you have the understanding of how to purchase and trade your penny stocks you will need to know how to track them in the system so that you can make a right decision on when to sell. Tracking your assets can be difficult, but due to the popularity of stocks, most companies have created excellent systems to track different stocks and all at the touch of your fingers.

CHAPTER FIVE
TRACKING YOUR PENNY STOCKS

Even if you don't decide to trade and play the exchange every day, you should at least take the time to track your stocks to prevent surprise drops in the market. You can set many different alerts on your online profiles, but it is still important to see what your stocks are doing and whether you need to make different choices than the alarms you have set for yourself. Sometimes stocks will go stagnant, and that may be a good time to go ahead and sell even if you haven't yet reached your twenty or thirty percent return because often that stagnant information precedes a drop in value for a stock. You also want to see how the stocks that you are tracking are performing to know whether they may be contenders once they reach their fifty-second week. Once you have down the research and purchase part of penny stocks, tracking truly becomes the most important aspect of playing the market.

Tracking stocks is a highly vital skill that will help increase your chances of profiting and maximizing your return on investment. The stock market fluctuates on an hourly basis, and because of that, you can turn profits into losses in the blink of an eye. Therefore it is pertinent to correctly track stocks with the knowledge of what each column represents and how it relates to your specific stock. If for some reason you are found without the use of the internet you can grab the newspaper and track assets from the previous day in the finance section. You also should be able to review most of the information we are providing in your online profile on your brokerage website. We will take the time in this chapter to discuss how to find the stock information, how to understand the information you are viewing, and how to look for patterns when you are tracking your investments.

Finding Your Stock Information

Before you can begin to track the stocks you have purchased and the ones you are considering for investment, you have to be able to find your stock information. The process, online, is relatively straightforward but without the knowledge of where and what to look for, you may find yourself searching through mounds of data. You want first to go into your personalized section of your firm's website where you do all of your purchasing and look for the tracking section of the site, or you can go online to the major news sites and track your stocks through there. You may end up doing a mixture of both depending on where you are and how much time you have to track. They also have started to make apps for your phone that will give you real-time data on the stock market, though some of them do not include penny stocks yet.

Symbols

The next thing you need to do in order to track your stocks is to figure out what the ticker symbol for your particular stocks are. The ticker symbol is a mixture of up to five letters that usually resembles the name of the company or its major product line. These abbreviations are how the stock market tracks each and every business in their system. An example of one of these symbols is Apple which has a ticker symbol of APPL. These symbols should be tracked at the time you choose to purchase them so writing them down will help eliminate this part. However, if you didn't write them down, you can quickly search for the name either in the database or by putting the search inquiry into Google or other search engines.

News Websites

Again, your brokerage site is not the only place to look up stock fluctuations and charts; major news websites usually have real-time displays of these numbers as well. To search, you would enter the ticker symbol in the search bar of the financial section of the website. Also, most internet browsers and search engines have a stock tracking system, and you can just enter the ticker symbol into the engine and get results immediately. If you are looking in the paper for the information, you would go to the finance section of the paper and look for the ticker symbol in the charts. Remember, though, penny stocks are not traded on the major markets so you may not be able to find your company in the paper since it usually focuses on the biggest movers on the market in that time period.

Your Online Brokerage Account

If you are able to get onto your brokerage account that will ultimately be the best place to view tracking information and you can usually change the settings to focus on your purchased stock. The current prices and the most recent trades should automatically be generated and show up on your home screen when you log on, though every website is different. Make sure to check out your broker's help section to get a thorough understanding of all of the additional tools they offer to better and more efficiently track your investments. If your account doesn't offer anything but the basis, you may want to add to another website that will allow you to use these particular tools or look up the cost to increase your membership in your current site.

Online Portfolios

One of the beautiful things about technology is that you don't have to worry about having thousands of sheets of paper in a real portfolio. Online portfolios are sometimes available through your brokerage page but sometimes you will have to create them from an outside source. If you have one of these portfolios, you should be able to log in, click on the tracker tool, enter your ticker symbol and have all the information you need to make educated choices on your investments. These portfolios also give you the capability of entering in stocks and their updated prices depending on how the market sways. Mint is a great online portfolio that is free and also includes an app for your smartphone so you can quickly track from anywhere.

Alerts

Alerts are going to be your best friend when you are playing the stock market but are unable to be watching your investments consistently. Not only should you set alerts for when stocks dip or your stocks rise or fall to a certain point, but you should also make sure to be informed if the companies you invested in end up in the news for any reason. Good news on a company can help you determine whether to extend you deadlines on specific stocks. Bad news about your business can signal that you need to get rid of the stock and quickly. If you are working in stocks that are affected by weather or exact conditions you should also program alerts for any of those issues as well. Unfortunately, natural events and developments in science can hurt companies, and you need to be aware of what is going on.

Understanding Stock Information

You can get alerts and pull up tracking information on your stocks all day long but if you don't understand what you are looking at it is not going to do you any good. You need to know the different stock information so that you are able to make informed decisions about your investments. Some of the tracking information is self-explanatory while other information can be confusing. Also, there is usually a link between all of the information and without individual statistics and information you may be missing an integral piece of the puzzle. When you are missing parts, it is very likely that you could make a mistake in trading that could cost you significant amounts of money. Again, as we have said through this whole book, educating yourself on all aspects of your investments is not only smart but can make the difference between maximizing your revenue and losing everything you put into it.

Interpreting Price Changes

When you are looking at the tracking information, you are going to see the high, low, and closing prices. These numbers indicate how the stock did, on average, for the prior day, the top, low, and final cost of the stock. The 52-week column is going to give you an excellent idea of how volatile that specific stock is. If the latter two prices have a large difference, then the odds are this stock has a greater opportunity for gain but a higher risk for loss. If the numbers are relatively close then that shows the stock as pretty conservative so you may not achieve as high but your likelihood of loss is less as well. The net change tells you the gain or loss of a specific stock for that twenty-four hour time period and is calculated by taking the previous day's closing cost and subtracting it from the current days. There is a plethora of information on this that can be found on the web.

Dividends

The dividends are going to tell you how much a company would pay you to hold one share of its stock for one year. This dividend might rise, fall, or be removed based on the enterprise's performance and status. If a company continually pays out dividends and increases those payouts over time, the company is considered a good choice to invest in. Dividends are either paid out to the shareholders or reinvested in the enterprise. If a company has a plan for substantial growth, they will usually not pay dividends while the businesses that aren't planning growth will pay out. If you are interested in knowing more about a company's dividend history you can calculate the payout ratio which will tell you how much the company has paid out to shareholders and how that has changed over time.

Price-To-Earnings Ratio

The PE ratio or price-to-earnings ratio is the closing price divided by the earnings of outstanding share and represents the investor confidence that the stock will go up in the future. A low price-to-earnings ratio would represent an underdeveloped company which could trigger a possible active investment to make. This rate primarily represents what an investor is willing to pay for one dollar of the current earnings. So for example, if the PE ratio sits at thirteen, then they are will to pay thirteen dollars for one dollar of the current earnings. Theses findings can sometimes be difficult to understand. A high PE means that the company is stable and there is a good chance the stock prices will rise while the low PE means the company has the potential to grow, also showing a possible rise in stock prices. To really understand where a company fits into its industry, compare PE ratios with similar businesses in the same field.

Trading Volume

The trading volume is very simple and represents the number of shares that was traded that day. An unusual increase in a trade's volume may indicate that it is either on the rise or getting ready to go into a slump, either way, research is needed before purchasing any of that stock. If the price increases with the increase in volume then usually that indicates that a stock will be on the rise and vice versa. The trading volume is also the number you will want to look at when you are ready to begin trading stock. It is important to not sell any more than ten or fifteen percent of the trading volume a day. This is a number you don't have to check every day but is pertinent to your choices in investment.

Ratings

Analysts will sometimes put ratings and price targets that show whether they believe the stock will rise or fall in the future. The ratings include buy, sell, or hold and tell investors what the analysts believe they should do with specific stocks. These ratings can easily be found on any of the major market watch sites but remember they are a guess, not information that you necessarily have to listen to and they could still go either way.

Looking For Patterns

A chart pattern is a particular movement in the stock charts that can be analyzed and used to predict how an individual stock will trend in the future. The information is based on current movement as compared to the past flow of that capital as well as the historical outcomes of similar charting paths. Chartists use this information to help investors decide whether they should buy, sell, or hold their current stock in that company. However, this is also a good skill to have when you are looking at your own businesses and deciding on whether to invest. Penny stocks may be hard to determine through patterns since they have limited information, but you can use it as you move into other stock options in the future. Predicting the movement of stocks is just a prediction, and you should never base your decision on whether to buy a stock or not solely on the charts and patterns you discover.

Know The Business

Stocks can be volatile, especially penny stocks, and tend to highly fluctuate over the course of a week so if you want to get a better idea of a stock's tendency, then you need to look at the stock over the process of a week or month and compare those numbers. If the stock has extreme highs and lows over that period, it may not be a stock you want to invest in since Penny stocks only stay with you for several days. You can also tend to find long-term financial stability by studying the company's financial records if they are available. If the penny stock is a new corporation, then this won't help you very much in determining the positivity of the investment.

Day-Trading

Day-trading highly focuses on the very short term for a stock and can be extremely high risk. Day traders run the risk of experiencing severe losses if their bids are incorrect or if the fees eat up all of their return on investment. Technically day traders bank on being able to read the patterns and understanding whether a particular stock will rise or fall but this is extremely hard to do in the short term, and many of these people lost quickly. Though investors in penny stocks aren't considered day traders they essentially do the same thing, look for patterns and buy and trade in a few day period. Day-trading is not recommended in any type of investment strategy, and you could run the risk of losing more than you put in, taking you backward in your pursuit of your goals.

Trends

The simplest type of pattern for anyone to analyze is the price trend. You want to look for growth and decline of a stock price over days or weeks. Remember that just because a stock had a trend in growth does not mean that in the next fifteen minutes it won't have significant loss. Another trend to discover is basing the stocks on economic trends and major news for a company which can both raise the stock price or even make it come crashing down. A good thing to do when studying trends is to take a compilation of these different numbers to base your decision on. However trends are like fortune telling for investors, you never know if you will make the right choice.

Support and Resistance

Support and resistance are two terms that investors use to point out the numbers in which a specific stock does not move below or above. For example, if you have a stock that routinely gets near or to $23, but never goes over it then it has a resistance of $23. Likewise, if a stock never goes under $12, then it has a support of $12. Understanding this trend and how to track it can help you identify the prices in which the chosen stock will not fall under or go over. When you are working with penny stocks, these numbers may not be available due to the amount of time the company had its shares on the market, but you can try to establish it with its last month of numbers at least.

Head and Shoulders

When we say head and shoulders, we are not talking about curing your dandruff. Instead, we are talking about an intricate pattern that investors and analysts use to determine stock shifts. The pattern is formed when the stock reaches a high, or the left shoulder, dips, reaches an even higher high, the head, dips, and then comes back up to a peak not as high as the head, giving you the right shoulder. This trend usually signifies the end of the upward trend of a stock, and it is then predicted to decline in price. In order to determine where you should sell the stock, you can draw a line between the two head points and it will identify the best location to get rid of the stock.

In this chapter, we discussed many pertinent things that will help you to understand the stock market and even help you predict the rise and fall of stocks. All of this information will become helpful somewhere in your investment journey even if you cannot use it in the penny stock industry. To further be able to invest time and money in your future you need to fully understand risk and the other investments to consider in order to diversify your portfolio.

CHAPTER SIX
UNDERSTANDING RISK

You are now at a point in your penny stock investments where you should know how to research, purchase, and trade like a pro. You will have come up with your own best practices by now and hopefully that is serving you well. We know that Penny stocks are high risk, but not all investments in your portfolio should be the same risk level. We will discuss the importance of a diversified portfolio in the last chapter of this book, but first, we need to break investments down a bit further. This information will help you in penny stocks and in the rest of your investments. There are so many different ways that you can invest your money for the future and to understand where they fit into your plan you must understand the importance of risk and how it affects your return on investments.

Risk can seem like a scary thing, especially when it comes to your money and your future but it is a necessary entity in order to make money on your investments. Risk is absolutely fundamental to the discussion of rates and returns, and without it, you won't have a reason to invest your money. The three types of risk we will be discussing in this chapter are low, medium, and high-risk investments. Don't let the words themselves turn you off; each one has a significant role to play when it comes to your financial goals and investments. This chapter will give you the understanding of what each risk means, why it is relevant to your portfolio, and a description of some of the most attractive investments in each category. Once you understand the risk, you can then move on to creating a robust and diversified portfolio. The stronger your portfolio, the quicker you will be reaching your financial and future goals.

Low-Risk

A low-risk investment is one that has a small, or low, chance of losing some or all of the money you have put forward. Low-risk investments, while the safest of all the investments, yield the lowest return out of all of the risk levels. Don't be fooled there is always a level of danger in every investment, and even though there is a small amount of risk associated with this type of investment, anything can happen. Low-risk investments are usually longer investments but also be considered something as simple as a high-yield savings account. Your banker or financial adviser will have a comprehensive list and description of every type of low-risk investment that is available in today's market. Many of the low-risk investments you will need the assistance of at least your local banker to start, and it's always good to speak to them ahead of time since these types of investments all are relatively similar and hard to push through sometimes.

You might be wondering why you would put a portion of your investment into something that is going to yield a small return and the answer is relatively straightforward. When you are spending larger portions of your expendable income on the medium and high-risk investments, you want to make sure that you have a backup. If something were to go wrong with your stocks and you lose all of the money you put into it, you are not completely at ground zero with your investments because you have a percentage of your money tied up in low-risk loans, just sitting there collecting returns. This, you will see later, is one of the key elements of a diversified portfolio. You want to backup your money with safely invested money for the future. Let's take a look at some of the most attractive low-risk investments.

Certificate Of Deposit

A Certificate of Deposit, or CD, you are depositing money for a specified amount of time in exchange for a guaranteed return on investment. You can find these low-risk investments through a credit union, broker or your bank. When you invest in a CD, you will be assigned a specific interest rate that is locked in and will not change regardless of the market. However, you are forced to keep that money in the bank, and if you choose to withdraw it early, you will pay the hefty penalty of three months worth of interest.

When you are investing in a CD you want to get one with a FDIC insured financial institution because this will guarantee in case of an economic catastrophe that you will get the principal back as long as it is less than $250,000. This ultimately tells you that the U.S. government is guaranteeing you will not take a loss, and the bank will pay you interest as well. The interest rates for CD's vary, and your specific rate will depend on the current interest rates and the amount of time you will invest your money for. Usually, the longer you set your CD up for, the higher the interest rate you will be offered. CD's are one of the safest, low-risk, investments on the market today.

Treasury Inflation Protected Securities

Treasury Inflation-Protected Securities, or TIPS, are a form of bond that the United States Treasury offers and is the lowest-risk bond there is. There are two methods of growth for these bonds, fixed interest rate, and built-in inflation protection. The fixed interest rate will stay constant for the length of the bond. The built-in inflation protection is a government guarantee that allows your investment value to grow whenever the rate of inflation grows during the period you hold the Treasury Inflation Protected Security.

To understand this imagine you invested in a TIPS that comes with a .25% interest rate which is really low. Since this interest rate is even lower than most savings accounts, the investment doesn't seem too appealing. However, if the inflation grows at a rate of 2% per year for the time period of the bond, your investment will also increase with inflation and result in a higher return. There are two ways you can purchase your TIPS, and that is individually, which allows you to pick your TIPS or through investment in a Mutual Fund that invests in TIPS, which is much easier to manage. Either way, this is an excellent way to invest in a government secured low-risk portfolio option and feel comfortable that regardless of how your other investments work out, there will be money saved in a safe position.

Medium-Risk

A medium-risk investment is one that has a relatively higher than low-risk, or medium, chance of losing some or all of the money you have put forward. Medium-risk investments, while not the safest but definitely not the riskiest of all the investments, yield good returns on investment. Don't be fooled there is always a level of risk in every investment, and even though this risk level is not the worst, it can teeter back and forth making investments dangerous sometimes. Medium-risk investments are usually longer investments but also take the most work by the investor and can be considered career changes at times. There are some investment strategies that are medium-risk that your banker or broker can help you with while others are things such as starting your own business. Medium-risk investments may take up more of the investor's personal time, but they can sometimes yield returns higher than high-risk investments.

You might not want to put money into an investment that will take up an exorbitant amount of time and that is okay, there are other options out there for medium-risk investments. However, you can't leave medium-risk investments out of your portfolio since they can yield higher returns while still sitting comfortably in the medium-risk area. If something were to go wrong with your high-risk stocks and you lose all of the money you put into it, you are not completely at ground zero with your investments because you still have your medium-risk investments bringing in returns and your low-risk investments simmering. Ultimately what you are doing is attempting to make more return for goals and backing up your money with other investments down the ladder. You are creating a protection system, so you don't end up completely tapped out if the market crashes. Let's take a look at some of the most popular medium-risk investments.

Preferred Stock

Preferred Stock is a security but it is complex, and it trades like stocks but reacts like a bond in several ways. The return rate is usually two percent higher than a Certificate of Deposit and deals within a few dollars of the issue price which is typically around $25 a share. The offerings for preferred stock pay either monthly or quarterly and their returns can sometimes qualify for capital gains treatment. This stock is exceptional since it has little to no liquidity risk and can be sold at any time. The two types of risks that preferred stocks seem to carry are the market and tax risks.

There are several different types of preferred stocks available. The Cumulative preferred accumulates returns the company can't pay due to economic issues. When the company catches up and becomes stable again, the past due returns are paid to the shareholder. Participating preferred stocks allow the holder to get larger returns if the company is on the up and up. Convertible preferred stock can be converted or changed into specific numbers of common stock. Either way, the shareholder of a preferred stock can always count on receiving their money back from the issuer before the company liquidates. However, they do not hold any voting rights.

Fixed Annuities

Fixed annuities are a very conservative medium-risk investment that usually is designed to focus on retirement savings that yield higher returns but with a middle of the road risk level. Fixed annuities are unique, and they allow you to an unlimited amount of money into them and then let it sit and grow tax-deferred until the time of retirement. Of course, if you are looking for a shorter-term investment this would not be the one for you, but depending on your timelines, this investment could be very helpful for you long term goals.

Fixed annuities can be purchased from life insurance companies, and the investment and return or interest is protected by that company as well as the state guaranty fund that reimburses you when you buy the contract from a company that can no longer pay out. As with any investment, there is a chance that you can lose your money due to bankruptcy, so it is important to choose a financially sound and insured company to purchase this contract from. Since this type of investment is relatively safe for a medium-risk investment, it only pays about one percent higher in returns than a Certificate of Deposit or security, but you can sometimes find higher introductory rates used to bring in investors. One of the major downsides to this type of investment are the substantial penalties paid if you were to withdraw your money early for any reason.

High-Risk

A high-risk investment is one that has a relatively large, or high, chance of losing some or all of the money you have put forward. High-risk investments, while presenting you with an unsecured method of investing, yields incredible returns on investment as long as the deal does not backfire. Don't let the idea of high-risk investments scare you away immediately; they are fickle but with the right education and guidance they can be just what you are looking for. High-risk investments can be short term like penny stocks or long term with regular stocks that you purchase and hold, riding the stock exchange waves. There are some investment strategies that are medium-risk that your banker or broker can help you with while others are things such as starting your own business. Almost all high-risk investments need the assistance of a financial advisor or broker to accomplish or guide you through the process safely as possible. High-risk investments may be shaky at best, but they can also make up the bulk of your financial return on investment if played right.

Like the other levels of risk, there are levels of high-risk investments as well. You don't have to go out guns blazing and invest your money in the riskiest company on the market in order to make high returns. You may be wary of diving into this area of your diversification, even with penny stocks under your belt.

However, you can't leave high-risk investments out of your portfolio since they can yield the highest returns on investment and could make or break your timeline in your financial plan. High-risk investments can play two different roles in your portfolio; they can save it after issue, and they can increase your rate of return exponentially. If you have medium-risk investments that fall through or have to be used in case of emergency high-risk investments can make that money back plus some in a relatively short period of time. Ultimately what you are doing is attempting to make more return for goals and backing up your money with other investments down the ladder while increasing your earning potential tenfold. You are creating a protection system, so you don't end up completely tapped out if the market crashes. Let's take a look at some of the most popular high-risk investments.

Leveraged Oil ETF's

Leveraged oil ETF's are some of the riskiest and volatile stocks on the market for several reasons. The ETF's are often traded in a high-volume capacity and are known for their high levels of volatility. However, due to this the leverage oil ETFs can bring you extreme returns, and losses if these are done hastily. The oil itself is extremely volatile in price and only adds to the danger of this high-risk investment. Played correctly, though, and you could see extreme return on investment.

Options

Options are primarily used by investors that are attempting to time the market and can yield high return on investment if used correctly. The investor who purchases the option usually also buys a stock or commodity equity for a particular price within a likely range of dates. If the price of the security ends up not being what the investor predicted it to be, they don't have to purchase or sell the option security. The risk behind this is extremely high since it puts time requirements on the acquisition or sale. This is usually discouraged by professionals since timing the market is regarded as volatile, but this is also why options can bring you extremely high returns on investment.

Initial Public Offerings

Initial Public Offerings, or IPOs, is the first time a company offers its stock to the public. Some of these stocks draw a lot of attention and can stagger valuations and professional judgments of offer on short-term returns. Other initial offerings are a lot less high-profile and offer you a chance to buy shares while the company is undervalued. This will then lead to higher short and long-term return on investment.

Initial Public Offerings are high-risk because regardless of the regulations by the SEC, there is always going to be a high level of uncertainty for new a new company. Investors worry that the management of the enterprise may not be able to do what is necessary to push the business forward to success. Though this stock is high-risk, the opportunity for returns is extremely high.

<u>Venture Capital</u>

Venture capital takes a considerable upfront investment, and the investment requires loaning money to parties who are creating brand new businesses. To be a venture capitalist you need to understand everything about the company that the possible client will be starting, their background, the product or service, and how you believe it will do in today's market. You can either fund the business on your own or go in as a partnership with other venture capitalists.

The risk for this type of investment is very high. The likelihood of a company exploding into today's market is microscopic, in fact, the probability of a company surviving isn't very good either. However, if you are successful and the company blossoms not only do you make a high rate of return but in most instances, you retain some long term control over the enterprise. The deals vary from capitalist to capitalist, but the risks are high, and the outcome can be huge or detrimental to your investments.

CHAPTER SEVEN
HAVING A SOLID AND DIVERSIFIED PORTFOLIO

Welcome to the last chapter in this book where we have given you the tools and education needed to dive into the world of penny stocks and rake in huge returns on investment. However, we couldn't just stop there. Instead, we are attempting to give you a solid grasp on the rest of your investment future. You just learned everything you need to know about the different general levels of risk and how they pertain to you and your portfolio. Going forward you will have to broaden your investments beyond penny stocks and come up with a plan that is multi-faceted and includes investments from all risk levels to make the financial goal you need while protecting your money from the top down. With these tools, you will not only succeed in your financial plan, but you will be able to broaden even further and create a sense of financial stability and freedom using the money you make from returns.

Now that we understand what the different levels of risk are and why they are relevant to your portfolio, we are going to end this book with the tools you will need to create a robust and diversified portfolio of investments. Before we give you each step to building this amazing portfolio, we are going to discuss why this is so important to your investment future. Designing your portfolio is not as difficult as it may seem and there are many tools on the internet that can simplify the process for you. If you are going to go with an online portfolio make sure you invest in a version that is going to be full and comprehensive, otherwise you may find yourself severely lacking in different areas of your investments. If you don't want to put the money out for the site, you can easily find templates and instructions all over the web for creating the perfect portfolio from scratch. Another option, a bit more expensive, is to have a financial agent build this portfolio for you. Let's begin by discussing the importance of a diversified portfolio.

The Importance Of Diversification In Your Portfolio

Diversification can be described as a technique that helps to reduce investment risk by placing investments throughout different instruments, industries, and categories. This structure is used to attempt to maximize your return on investment because if you are invested in various unlinked markets, one may be affected, but the others will not be. Almost every professional in the financial business agree that diversification is the most important piece of the puzzle for reaching financial goals with minimized risk, both long and short.

If we look at an example of diversification such as putting all of your investments into the automotive business you can see how if several companies fold or gas powered vehicles are outlawed your investments will plummet and you will be left with nothing. However, if you spread these investments out among different companies, markets, and genres when the automotive industry takes a dive your other investments will stay firm. To achieve the highest level of diversification in your portfolio you need to spread these investments across the board. There are numerous ways out there today to add more diversification to your investments, but a lot of them are difficult for new or intermediate investors to understand. Professionals still believe that bonds are one of the best steps towards diversifying your portfolio. Along with these bonds, many people will choose to diversify through stocks but how many stocks is too many? There is a fine line when it comes to playing the stock market, and while five shares are better than one, there is a bit of confusion among professionals about how many different stocks you should have before they no longer make a difference. Most of these investors say that fifteen to twenty different stocks across a broad range of industries is an excellent way to diversify and reduce risk while still holding on to high returns.

Steps To Building An Amazing Portfolio

Today's financial investing market requires a strong, well-maintained, diversified portfolio in order to be successful. Beyond just making sure you include investments from all walks of the financial industry, you also need to decide the best asset allocation that will follow your personal investment goals and strategy. Your portfolio should be catered to general safety and risk management while also being fit for your own choices and investments. There is an approach that investors can take that can help them reach this portfolio goal while maintaining their investing strategy integrity. This section is aligned with that strategy and will help you take the steps you need to build that amazing portfolio you are looking for. With a robust personalized approach, you are going to not only reach your goals but bring back an enormous return on investment, something you set out to do in the first place. Let's take a good look at these vital four steps.

Asset Allocation

Understanding and holding on to your personal financial goals and investment plan is the first thing you need to accomplish when you are constructing your portfolio. There are several different things you need to consider including time goals for investment growth, your age, and the amount of expendable income you need to invest to get to the volume of money you need in the future. All of these variables play a huge part in your plan since a young college student, and a sixty-year-old will have two different ideas for their financial future and their goals.

Another aspect to take into account is your personality and tolerance at risk. Sometimes taking high risks at the expense of your mental status may not be worth the returns. If you are reaping superior returns but you lose concentration and sleep every time one of your stocks takes a dip in the market you might want to rethink your risk strategy. You may want those quick high returns, but if your days are filled with stress, you may find yourself making poor investment choices or even pulling out of your financial plan altogether. The point of a strategy is to make it workable in a way that fits your life, not completely flipping your life upside down.

Discovering your risk tolerance, understanding your current financial standing, and knowing what you will need for the future is vital information that you will use to determine how to allocate your investments. Besides the second chapter where we discussed preparation, we have really focused on the technicals up to this point. However, your personal aspects need to be inputted into your financial strategy otherwise your investments will not line up with your current and plans. The risk/return tradeoff plays a vital part in your success. This is the theory that greater gains come at the expense of increased risk of loss, and that needs to be personalized to your preferences. Remember, there is no such thing as zero risks in the investment arena, so you need to be realistic and not let your fears override your plan too much. However, your place in life will determine how lenient you can be in the risk taking the field. That college student who isn't relying on the returns to live can take more risk than the sixty-year-old who is getting ready to live off of their assets.

In a nutshell, use your personal life and goals to dictate how you will plan out your investment strategy. Don't be too risky when your lifestyle dictates the need to protect your assets. However, take a little bit of a chance if your goals don't include living off of your returns anytime soon. Make your plan a substantial reflection of you and your future.

Conservative or Aggressive?
Ultimately your portfolio will show how much risk you can take on and the more that is, the more aggressive investments you will take on. You will have a significant portion of your investments going to average and high-risk investments and the smaller

portion to things like bonds and Certificates of Deposit. On the other hand, the less risk your life can handle, the less competitive your investment structure will be. A conservative portfolio might have less medium and high and more low-risk investments. If you are a conservative investor we might see your fixed income securities sitting at seventy to seventy-five percent, your equities at fifteen to twenty percent, and your cash and assets at five to fifteen percent. On the other hand, an aggressive investor might have fifty to fifty-five percent in equities, thirty-five to forty percent in fixed income securities, and five to ten percent in cash.

The primary goal of a conservative portfolio would be to protect its current assets, receive current income from bonds, but still leave some room for growth investments and the ability to reinvest in other areas. The primary goal of an aggressive portfolio would be to project a middle of the ground or high-risk tolerance, and balance that with capital growth. Even the most aggressive investor still must take the time to diversify their portfolio and leave room for fluctuations and pitfalls in the market. The point of investing for each person is different, but the primary goal for any investments is to put your money to work making returns that you can use towards your future goals. No one but you knows what type of risk tolerance you have or what you want out of your investments in the end, but it is important to follow your own guidelines and not take any additional risk that isn't necessary.

There are many different tools you can access to assess your risk tolerance really, but it definitely needs to be something you account for each and every time you adjust your portfolio. It is not recommended to throw caution to the wind and just put all of your money into risky but profitable investments, especially when the money that is being invested is also the money you will be using to live on. Also remember that investments are always made privy to the wonderful world of taxes, so you need to be prepared to owe taxes when you begin cashing investments in for use on your goals, you don't want to be left short of your goal because you forgot to factor in taxes and fees.

Achieving Your Perfect Portfolio

When you have finally determined the ideal asset allocation for your personal portfolio, you then need to divide your money between the appropriate asset classes simply. The asset classes on the surface are simple as equities and bonds, but those classes can and should be broken down further into subclasses. These subclasses will have different risks and returns and should fit with your personal investment strategy. There are several different strategies you can implement when you are deciding on the assets and securities for your allocation in your portfolio.

Choosing Stocks- You want to analyze the corporations and screen stocks to put them on your list of possible choices. It is important to choose stocks that are the level of risk that you want in your equity portion of your portfolio. You should also consider the market cap, stock type, and sector when you are picking these investments. Once you have shortlisted several options that is when you implement that research we have been discussing throughout this book. These are the most labor intensive investments and require you to track, monitor, and pay attention to the company, the country, and the market on a regular basis.

Choosing Bonds- Bonds are less stressful to choose since they are all relatively safe and all fall under your low-risk category. When you are deciding on what bonds you want to invest in make sure to look at the coupon, maturity, rating, type, and the general interest rate. Match those things up with your strategy and the choice should be simple.

Mutual and Index Funds- Mutual funds allow you to hold stock and bonds that have been professionally researched and hand picked by managers. These funds require a fee to the manager, but they are relatively safe and give an average return on investment. Your other option is an Index fund which has lower costs and is not managed firmly. They are an excellent alternative to Mutual funds but don't expect the same type of return on investment.

Exchange-Traded Funds (ETFs) - ETFs are great alternatives to Mutual Funds and Index Funds and is basically a Mutual fund that is traded like a stock. The are similar because they represent a broad basket of inventory, but they are not actively managed. The stocks are usually grouped together by sector, capital, country, etc. and offer a lower price than mutual funds. Because of Exchange-Traded Fund's diversity, they make excellent additions to a portfolio that needs a little extra love in the diversification field. You would usually invest in ETFs instead of mutual funds not along with them.

Reassess And Rebalance

Once your portfolio is established and running, it is important to reassess and rebalance it on a quarterly basis since the market moves, and shifts and that can affect your initial weights in each class. To do this, you want to categorize your investments and then determine the value proposition as a whole system. You also need to understand that your current finances may change, your future goals may shift, and your risk tolerance may move between quarters so you may need to adjust your portfolio according to the changes. If your risk tolerance becomes lower, your equities need to follow suit and vice versa. Remember, as your tolerance goes up you can explore riskier options such as small-cap stocks.

Once you have determined the value position, you need to then figure out which of your positions are over and under weighted. You need to determine how much you need to reduce and what to allocate to other classes. Then you need to figure out how much of the underweighted securities you need to purchase and how much of the overweight you need to sell. You can buy the under with the profit of the overweight. To buy the new items for your portfolio, you repeat the buying process as usual. However, when you are looking at rebalancing you also need to take into consideration any tax implications you may incur. If your investments in stocks have gone up over the year and you sell all of your equity to rebalance you are going to incur some serious capital gains taxes. If this is the case rebalancing will just take a little bit longer. You will need to leave everything as is and instead of contributing to all your sectors, you will leave that particular one alone while adding to the others. Eventually, it will weight itself back out. However, if you think those stocks may be ready to fall selling them despite the tax implications may be the wisest move. You should consult analytics and research to help you decide what the outlook for your particular stocks are.

Monitoring your portfolio can keep you from getting behind on your goals by investing in the wrong categories and having an unbalanced risk assessment can be detrimental to your returns. Just because something is making money doesn't mean you shouldn't change it if your circumstances change. Most likely, when you adjust, you are doing it for the betterment of your investments, and you will see that pay off in your returns. Make smart, educated choices for your portfolio understanding it is what will fuel your future financial goals.

Creating a diversified portfolio is a highly vital part of reaching your financial and personal goals. Without diversification, you are setting yourself up for severe losses and possibly debilitating destruction of your current and fiscal future. Understanding your portfolio, how to successfully decide on risk tolerance, and allocation of equities is a must have for your portfolio, in fact, it makes your investment strategy what it is and what it will be. Once you are on your way with your investments, don't forget to reevaluate your portfolio on a regular basis in order to keep up with the ever-changing market, your financial changes, and the evolution of goals, both long term and short. You will see that as you reach your short term goals your portfolio will need to be reassessed and rebalanced in order to stay on track with the aims you have not yet made. A strategic and intelligent plan of attack and strategy is needed in order to have the perfect balance of your portfolio which will ultimately bring you the highest rate of return on investment that you can acquire from your personal investment strategy.

CONCLUSION

First, we would like to extend our thanks again for your purchase of *Jump Start Your Road To Riches--Maximize Your Profits With Penny Stock Trading*. We hope that you found this book informative and inclusive on your travels through investments. Congratulations on taking hold of your future and starting your investing with Penny Stocks as a strategic way to maximize your savings and push forward towards your future goals. Making a commitment to investing and a strong portfolio is an excellent choice and will help you in your future whether you are retiring, planning a financial road to freedom, or looking forward to traveling the world. You may not make your first million off of Penny Stocks alone but the tools we have given you to understand penny stocks will transverse into the rest of your investment opportunities in the future and allow you to maximize your return on any investment.

At the beginning, you may have found that the world of investments and the amount of choices that you have was incredibly daunting and difficult to maneuver your way through but we hope that has been cleared up by now. Penny stocks are great ways to dip your toes into playing the stock market but with smaller risks and lower upfront financial requirements. Though we have learned that Penny Stocks are high risk but with smaller financial investments and there are numerous other options in the investment world, you always want to find the best tricks and strategy to get every penny from your investments. This book has given you the tools and know-how that will allow you to maneuver through the Penny stock arena confidently. The tips, tricks, and informative information has also enabled you to maximize your returns from your penny stocks which will increase your earning potential, move your goals forward, and diversify your investment portfolio, all while giving you excellent preliminary experience in the stock buying and trading industry.

You cannot start any type of investment without a thorough understanding of where your money is going and how exactly the process works. This book started off by giving you the ins and outs of Penny Stocks and what they specifically cover. You then got a brief history of the stocks and how they compare to stocks on all of the major markets that you see streamed hourly. The who's, what's, where's, why's and when's of Penny Stocks were explained and should have enabled you to intelligently and responsibly start your journey in the Penny Stock market. Even though these stocks are considered high-risk, your money is being invested in a way that you can maximize your return, new worth, and reach your goals at a faster pace than traditional savings options. With the information, we provided you should be able to go forth and make informed decisions on your personal investment strategy.

This book has also shown that there are many ways to invest your capital, but it is not always necessary to hire a financial planner or broker to do work that you could do yourself. With Penny stocks the fees for these professionals usually, eat up all of the profit you make. You have been given the knowledge to understand the system and where your money goes when it is invested. We thoroughly discussed brokers, representatives, and financial advisors so that you would know who and where to go when the time came to enlist professional assistance. We ended this chapter by explaining why it was important not to jump into penny stocks or any other investment without first taking the time to prepare yourself, your finances, and your strategies for investing. The preparation phase is literally one of the most important aspects of a diverse and useful portfolio.

It should be said and said again, which is why we are repeating it, that you should never jump into any investment without thorough research and always have a budget and goal plan done before any investments are made. The process of preparation always seems to loom over investors heads, but we showed in this chapter that you could do it and do it without pricey brokers. If you do choose to hire assistance you should first attempt the process on your own and use the professional for cleanup of the finished product. The information you needed to set up a functional and comfortable investment plan was discussed in detail in Chapter Two. There is a step by step instruction and template for completing your budget, financial and investment plan and how to set up your goals in a realistic and functional manner. Preparation should never be skipped as a lack of history, and plans can lead to loss of returns and poor choices in investments.

Preparation doesn't just mean you are going to be setting up a list of things to do for the future, training counts towards the things you need to do in the present to get to an investable position for the future. Chapter two also discussed what your current financial status should resemble before you start using money that may not be expendable. We gave you a thorough understanding of why it is important to have a savings account set up for an emergency fund that equates to at least six months, preferably a year, worth of your bills so that in the case of an emergency you are not left dismantling your investments. Going into your portfolio with a stable financial footing is an excellent way to maximize every dollar you have to invest, even if you are only venturing into Penny stocks. This chapter's information is vital to the long-term functionality of your portfolio and your investment strategy for the future.

After we had made sure that you understood Penny stocks, their functionality on a daily and weekly basis, and perfected your preparation routine to the point in which all investments are feasible, we walked right into purchasing your first stock. Because there are so many different sites that offer Penny Stock services, and due to their newly popular forum for high returns, we gave you a comprehensive overview of some of the most attractive and functional financial brokerage sites for trading Penny Stocks. There are so many options that one can get lost and you need to know you are picking the right location for you and your needs. From there we gave you an understanding of what types of stocks you should work with and how to maximize the return on investment no matter what share you hold and how long you plan to keep.

Once you picked your website and became comfortable with the forum, we talked about how to move beyond click and buy and move into deeply researched choices that will maximize your return on investment. You learned how to choose a stock that fit both your investment strategy and your risk level. It is now very clear that no matter how many stock you pick, each and every one of them needs to be personally researched ahead of time to make sure they are a good fit for you. We gave ample informative dialogue on opposing sides of the Penny Stock industry and how it is often riddled with fraud. Having an intense research process and not giving into "tips' from emails, calls, and newsletters will afford you higher dividends and more return in the end. Watching your stocks is important as well to understand when to sell.

The stock market is all around you throughout the day whether it is scrolling on the news, in your financial section of your paper, or at the top of your screen on the internet. Many of those stocks take a lot of preparation to trade but fortunately due to the lack of regulations; Penny Stocks can be quick and painless. Through training on how to recognize when it is time to sell a stock and how to read patterns, you will not need to deplete your returns by hiring a broker to trade your Penny Stocks. Understanding timing and knowing the signs that will lead you to sell your stocks is paramount and can play a key factor in the maximization of your money but can also, if done incorrectly, can lose you money quickly. You were given the basic strategy of timings and patterns before we dove into the actual act of trading.

When you have mastered the understanding of when to trade your stocks you are ready to review your investments and decide on a course of action. When that course of action leads to trade you want to be prepared to do so quickly but intelligently. We showed that even in the Penny Stock market stock levels can change in the blink of an and eye and knowing when to pull the plug can save you enormous amounts of money. You were informed of the importance of stops and how to avoid falling victim to extreme losses when you are unable to track the stock minute to minute. Many of us are not day traders, so life, family, and work continued around us as we work the system for our future. Glamor doesn't pay the bills and buying and trading because it seems like gold can leave you with dust in your account.

Once you have purchased and sold, you want to make sure you are tracking your investments. Tracking is something that we want to pay attention to but not let it take over our lives. You want to pay attention to how your stocks are working in the system without being worried to leave the screen for ten minutes. You can enable your website to alert you to a plethora of things including stock decline, natural disasters that could affect your company, newsworthy information about a company, and legal attributes that may have an impact on the outcome. We gave you the tools to successfully track your stocks, multiples at once when you are investing in different areas of the business.

Organization of your portfolio and your investments is one of the key things that will help you maximize your returns and keep you on the up and up with new and exciting investments.

Risk is involved in every type of investment even down to savings accounts, though their risk is very low. You may consider Penny Stocks as a low-risk investment because you are working with minuscule amounts of money per stock, but a risk is more about the opportunity to lose your investment then it is the worth of your inventory. You will find that Penny Stocks can be temperamental because you are working with startups and companies recovering from bankruptcy. Don't lose the motivation to handle your stocks any less carefully because their net worth is small; all those pennies will add up. Never underestimate the earning potential of a company and when you feel that, through research and understanding of the company's financial growth, the stock will continue to grow, there is no requirement that you trade it or cash out. However you want to play the market smart and look for a reasonable twenty to thirty percent return, not letting yourself get out of hand and wait for larger yields, the results can be disastrous.

We then lunged head first into the often intimidating area of tracking full force. You can't track well if you don't know what the different parts of the market stand for. We broke down the most important parts of the tracking system and gave a comprehensive understanding that can be utilized on even the major stock exchanges. You were made familiar with many different areas of the stock market so that you will be able to make smart choices and maximize your return on investment. Once you have mastered the ability to track your stocks comprehensively, you then needed to find the right avenue to do so. We then discussed the different sites you can use to track stocks, including how to read your local paper to get the prior day's numbers if you don't have access to the internet.

In this chapter, we maneuvered out of learning how to translate the information on the screen to real-time data and moved into a review of the different sites that you can use to track your investments. You may find that the location you use to trade is the place you are most comfortable tracking your investments but don't stop there. There are a plethora of avenues that will help you get ample information on a minute to minute basis, and you should utilize those to make informed decisions. We taught you to use all available tools to help you with your tracking and remember that a lot of the different sites offer assistance and educational tools that will help you actually develop your skills in the stock market.

By this point in the book, you have learned what Penny Stocks are, how to prepare yourself for your investment opportunity, how to purchase and trade Penny stocks and ultimately how to track them to maximize your return on investment. The last chapter focused on life after Penny stocks and how to diversify your portfolio while staying in your comfort zone with risk. As stated earlier Penny stocks are an incredible way to invest small amounts of money, learn the system, and educate yourself on the stock market but they should not be the end of your investment strategy. Diversifying and building your portfolio is crucial in order to protect yourself against loss, make the financial goals you have set out to reach, and ensure yourself a financial freedom that you desire. Portfolio diversification can be done on your own, or you can also invest in financial assistance from a firm or your bank to help you make the smartest decisions for the future of your investments.

This section of the book gave you a strong, informed understanding of what diversification mean and how to achieve that when building your portfolio. We also talked about why this is so important and how to build your portfolio with the correct weight in each different type of investment. The preceding chapter gave you play by play on the various levels of risk, why they are important, and examples of the various investments underneath these risks and the information will be used to create your portfolio. We gave you not only the tools to be successful with Penny Stocks but the ability to build a well balanced, personalized portfolio that you can use to go further into the investment world and bring more gain to your invested capital. Lastly, we gave you the information on how to reassess and rebalance your portfolio as the days and weeks progressed, and your life and the market shifted and moved.

Beginning your investment adventure or your stock experience with Penny Stocks is an incredibly smart and safe way to ease yourself into the stock exchange while earning returns on some of the most volatile stocks on the market. You may have started out by looking at the small value of each share, but you should now understand how to use bulk, research, and the system to turn those pennies into dollars. Always keep ahold of the understanding that your relationship with the stock market will be tumultuous and rocky, but if you follow the systems laid out for you, you should be able to ride those waves into a set of healthy and robust returns. Educate, research, and play the system smartly, and you will see more gains than losses as you maneuver through the system.

We would like to thank you again for purchasing *Jump Start Your Road To Riches--Maximize Your Profits With Penny Stock Trading* and hope that your future with investing is robust and bright. Make sure to use the information we have given you here to guide you through your investment adventures. Always ask questions and use the plethora of information available to you through your brokerage firm and other financial institutions. Good luck and if you enjoyed this book, please leave a review so others may reap the benefits of investing in the Penny Stock industry.

www.ingramcontent.com/pod-product-compliance
Lightning Source LLC
Chambersburg PA
CBHW070039210526
45170CB00012B/539